# Montana
## impressions

FARCOUNTRY
PRESS

photography by **John Reddy**

*Front cover:* The sapphire-blue waters of Lake Sherburne in Glacier National Park.

*Back cover:* A rainbow arcs over Medicine Rocks State Park in eastern Montana.

*Title page:* The picturesque Swan Range reflects in mirror-like Rainy Lake in the Seeley-Swan Valley.

*Right:* Willows hug the banks of French Creek southwest of Anaconda, a lush foreground that gives way to grassy open country. Timbered foothills surrender to the lofty peaks of the Anaconda-Pintler Wilderness southwest of Anaconda.

ISBN 10: 1-56037-484-5
ISBN 13: 978-1-56037-484-8

© 2009 by Farcountry Press
Photography © 2009 by John Reddy

For more information about our books, write Farcountry Press, P.O. Box 5630, Helena, MT 59604; call (800) 821-3874; or visit www.farcountrypress.com.

Created, produced, and designed in the United States.
Printed in China.

*Left:* Ribbons of warm color float through the sky at dawn, reflecting in Lake McDonald in Glacier National Park.

*Below:* A black wolf splashes through the North Fork of the Flathead River.

*Right:* Hay bales rest in this pastoral scene in the Little Blackfoot River Valley. Short growing seasons and long winters make hay a valuable commodity for the state's stockgrowers.

*Below:* Wheel tracks sweep toward an abandoned barn and outbuilding gilded by the day's last rays of sunshine. This old homestead is near central Montana's small rural community of Hobson.

*Right:* A colorful bouquet of summer flowers along the Rocky Mountain Front.

*Facing page:* The Centennial Mountains and last winter's snow stand guard over a verdant wildflower-dotted meadow. This range stretches across the Montana/Idaho border west of Yellowstone National Park. The fabulous views are well worth the seasonal trek over a long, gravel road.

*Right:* A rippling pond and dynamic summer sky east of Baker. Beauty is not limited to mountains and forests but resides in all corners of the state, including this rural area on Montana's eastern edge.

*Below:* Water jumps from rock ledge to rock ledge, cascading downward in this slow shutter-speed shot at Giant Springs State Park near Great Falls.

*Facing page:* Autumn wetland plants and grasses frame a small body of water southwest of Anaconda.

*Below:* Fallen aspen leaves nearly conceal a small creek in the Sheepshead Mountain area north of Butte—a contrast of colors, textures, and degrees of permanence.

*Above, left and right:* An American Indian bedecked in full regalia dances during the Blackfeet Indian Reservation's North American Indian Days in Browning, Montana. Intricate, colorful, and symbolic artwork adorns the costumes of dancers young and old.

*Facing page:* A pictograph is worth a thousand questions. Who were the people that lived here approximately 300 years ago and what were their lives like? This handprint and other pictographs are located in Bear Gulch west of Grass Range.

*Right:* Thousands of snow geese take to the air at Freezeout Lake, a resting spot for birds in spring and late fall during their biennial migration. Bird watchers also flock to this avian paradise northwest of Great Falls.

*Below:* A bull bison in Yellowstone National Park trudges through the snow. When moving through deep snow, bison swing their massive heads from side to side, clearing a path like a snowplow and exposing their forage.

*Right:* The Swan River National Wildlife Refuge on a misty autumn morning. The distant Swan Range and its mosaic of green and yellow are veiled by an ephemeral mist.

*Below:* Mule deer are prevalent across the state and are often seen in urban areas.

*Above:* An expansive view of deep-green fields and endless sky stretches beyond Canyon Ferry Road near Helena, just one of many vistas that illustrate Montana's nickname of "Big Sky Country."

*Inset:* A coyote in Yellowstone National Park, alert to its next opportunity.

*Right:* The sun's rays spotlight Grinnell Point as waves roll over the beach of Swiftcurrent Lake in Glacier National Park.

*Far right:* Western Montana's Swan Valley and Swan Range are two of the state's jewels. Here, the lush wetland environment of the outlet of Holland Lake provides wildlife habitat as well as outstanding scenery.

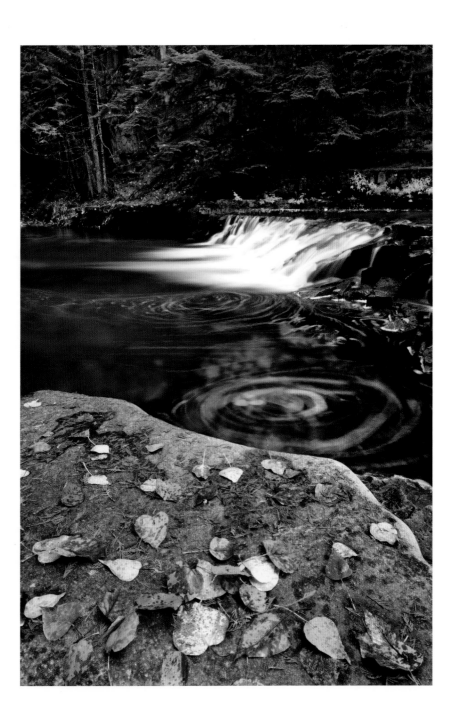

*Left:* Fall leaves caught in an eddy create a swirl of yellow in the dark waters at Ross Creek Giant Cedars southwest of Libby. The magic of these 500-year-old trees transports those who stroll among these giants to another time.

*Far left:* A cyclist sits on the dock of Lake McDonald in Glacier National Park. There are many ways to travel and treasure moments of serenity in Montana.

*Facing page:* There's a lot of horsepower in Montana. These spirited horses are kicking up dust in Gallatin Canyon near Bozeman.

*Below:* Cowboy ready to rope and ride.

*Right:* Rock Creek near Missoula in early fall.

*Facing page:* An alluring blaze of color adorns a grove of cottonwood trees south of Cardwell.

*Left:* Looking toward the Gates of the Mountains at sunrise, a spectacular scenic area near Helena where the Missouri River threads through a narrow passage of towering limestone cliffs.

*Far left:* A new day's promise at Salmon Lake northeast of Missoula, one of Montana's beautiful state parks.

*Right:* The resplendent colors of Yellowstone National Park's Grand Canyon are composed of sulphur, iron, and other minerals brought to the surface by geothermal activity. A slice of the park along its northern and western boundaries is within Montana.

*Far right:* Grand Prismatic Spring in Midway Geyser Basin, located in Yellowstone National Park's interior. A rainbow of hues created by microscopic bacteria rings the hot spring, resembling a painter's palette of color.

Shades of blue, gray, and white dominate a winter ranch scene east of Ovando. The snow-covered high country in the background is the Scapegoat Wilderness along the Continental Divide.

*Above:* Graceful lines in corn lily (false hellebore) leaves, Glacier National Park.

*Above, top:* Which is more beautiful: the blanketflower or the matching spider?

*Left:* Blooming bear grass crowds the valley floor like earthly stars while Glacier National Park's towering peaks, Mount Oberlin and Mount Cannon, stand guard.

*Above:* A golden wheat field in southwestern Montana, with the Tobacco Root Mountains in the distance.

*Left:* Autumn on the Missouri River at "Decision Point" near Loma. When the Lewis and Clark Expedition came to two forks in the river in early June 1805, they had to make a decision. After lengthy debate, Captains Meriwether Lewis and William Clark correctly identified and followed their desired waterway, the Missouri River.

*Right:* Frost shrouds native yucca, grasses, and cottonwood trees while fog engulfs the Missouri River's low country. It is a quiet and peaceful beginning to a new day.

*Far right:* The Big Belt Mountains and Canyon Ferry Lake are dressed in tonal pinks and blues during a frigid 20 below zero dusk.

*Left:* Dressed in lights at night, Helena's fire tower, or "Guardian of the Gulch," is an official city landmark. It stands as a reminder of the city's fiery past.

*Left, bottom:* Soft light illuminates the windows of St. Wenceslaus Church in the small town of Danvers in central Montana.

*Facing page:* Kelly's Saloon in the ghost town of Garnet, seen below a band of star trails captured by time-lapse photography.

*Right:* Swiftcurrent Creek at sunrise in the Many Glacier Valley, Glacier National Park.

*Far right:* The bare bones of nature are revealed in the Terry Badlands, especially at dawn and dusk. Layer upon layer of sedimentary rock change color as light washes over them, varying their mood throughout the day.

*Right:* Hungry Horse Dam on the South Fork of the Flathead River near Columbia Falls.

*Below, left:* A young boy learns the basics of fly fishing on the Sun River west of Great Falls.

*Below, right:* Whitewater kayaking is a favorite Montana pastime. Here, kayakers negotiate fast water on the Gallatin River.

*Right:* A jack-leg fence and dirt road west of Augusta sashay toward the Rocky Mountain Front at first light.

*Far right:* The brilliant fall colors of aspen and underbrush are mirrored in the Blackfoot River west of Lincoln.

*Facing page:* Montana cowgirls and their horses romp through the water.

*Below, left:* Father and son, similarly clad in typical ranch attire.

*Below, right:* A young girl gently rubs the neck of her horse.

*Right:* A beaver lodge on the edge of the Big Hole Valley's Miner Lake, adorned with floating lily pads and surrounded by lodgepole pine.

*Below:* Bull moose in velvet, Yellowstone National Park.

*Facing page:* A blooming garden spells "Montana" and greets visitors to the Montana State Capitol in Helena.

*Below, left:* Life-size bronze statues of Mike and Nancy Mansfield honor Montana's most revered statesman and his wife inside the Montana State Capitol.

*Below, right:* The beautiful interior of the Montana State Capitol highlights history and artful craftwork. The building was completed in 1902 and was renovated in 2000.

*Right:* Western Montana's Clark Fork River mirrors the high country. An otter interrupts the stillness of the shadowy blue water.

*Below, left:* A male wood duck is adorned with eye-catching and colorful plumage.

*Below, right:* A female mallard preens her feathers; though her color is subtle, she sports intricate patterns on her wings and back.

*Left:* The warm kiss of sunrise begins to fall on one of the most photographed scenes in Montana: Glacier National Park's towering peaks and Wild Goose Island in St. Mary Lake.

*Below:* A portrait of the delicate fairyslipper (also known as calypso orchid). On the trail, this flower peeks out from shade and beckons hikers to stoop low and look; its beauty is fleeting and worth the pause.

*Right:* A sandstone rock formation catches last light at Medicine Rocks State Park in southeastern Montana. These towering sculptures of sandstone have been whittled by time, wind, and weather and are considered by some American Indians to be "big medicine."

*Below:* Egg-shaped caprocks on a throne of softer, eroding stone in the badlands of Makoshika State Park near Glendive. A harsh landscape of intriguing pinnacles, hogback ridges, and fluted hills, the country is a dynamic lesson in geology. Note the tiny bluebird atop the point at far left in the foreground.

Sleek windmills near Judith Gap. Montana's wide-open spaces are good candidates for capturing passive energy.

*Right:* The sun begins to warm the Beartooth Range in south-central Montana, a magnificent wilderness of high peaks, alpine lakes, glaciers, and sweeping plateaus.

*Far right:* Pictograph Cave National Historic Landmark near Billings is also a state park.

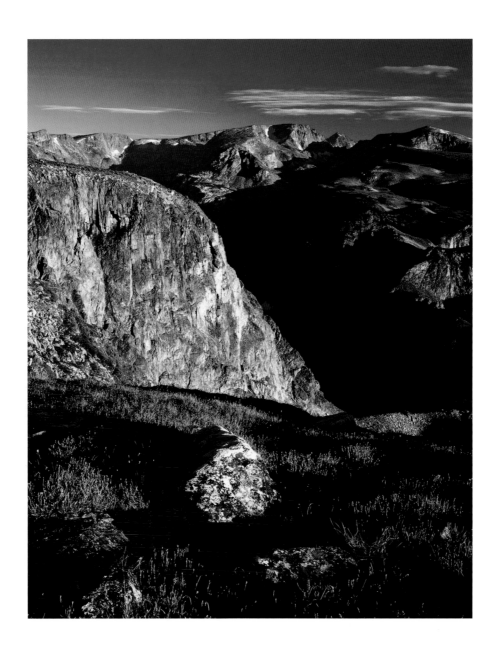

*Facing page:* A bobcat kitten explores its territory in late summer.

*Below:* The grizzly bear, perhaps the best symbol of an intact ecosystem. Two regions support this large mammal in the state, the Greater Yellowstone Ecosystem and the Northern Continental Divide Ecosystem near Glacier National Park.

*Above:* The town of Polson is situated at the southern end of northwestern Montana's Flathead Lake, the largest freshwater lake west of the Mississippi River. The Mission Mountains provide a stunning backdrop.

*Inset:* A red-tailed hawk rests atop a fir tree. This raptor is the state's most common hawk and is readily glimpsed during the day.

*Right:* Tepee poles reach for the sky at Big Hole National Battlefield, a site near the Idaho border in southwestern Montana where the U.S. Army led a surprise attack on the Nez Perce Indians in 1877. The army pursued the fleeing Nez Perce for months, finally defeating them in northern Montana.

*Below:* Within the boundaries of the Crow Indian Reservation in southeastern Montana, the Little Bighorn Battlefield National Monument memorializes June 25, 1876, when the U.S. Army's 7th Cavalry was overwhelmingly defeated by Lakota Sioux, Cheyenne, and Arapaho warriors.

*Above:* Paddlers love the rising sandstone walls that frame the Smith River in central Montana. A popular recreational river in summer, the Smith River begins in the Little Belt Mountains and ultimately empties into the Missouri River.

*Inset:* A fly fisherman rows to a favorite fishing hole on the Smith River.

*Facing page:* The Lamar River winds away from the Absaroka Range in Yellowstone National Park during a winter sunset full of surreal blues and pinks.

*Below, left:* A fallen leaf temporarily frozen in time on Canyon Ferry Lake.

*Below, right:* The last, lustrous light of a winter day lingers on the Big Belt Mountains in west-central Montana.

*Right:* The dazzling, bright-gold colors of the western larch tree, a deciduous conifer that sheds its needles each fall, are reason enough to embark on a trip to western Montana in October. Here, Lower Stillwater Lake reflects this temporary color.

*Below:* A bull elk bugles in fall, sending a strained, high-pitched wail into the air. Bull elk expend vocal energy to attract cow elk and challenge other males in the proximity of their harems.

*Right:* A reflected sunset in the pools of Great Fountain Geyser, Yellowstone National Park.

*Below:* An awe-inspiring Helena sunrise.

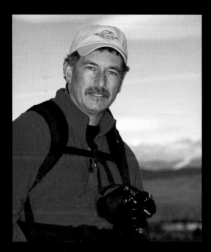

**JOHN REDDY** holds a degree in photography from Montana State University, where he later lectured for two years. His work has been extensively published in Montana and around the nation. John's photographs appear regularly in *Montana Magazine* and have been published in *Popular Photography, American Heritage, Sunset, Montana Living, Men's Journal, National Geographic Books, Outside, American Photo, Smithsonian Guide to Historic America,* and others. John's photography is featured in the Compass American (Fodor's) Guide *Montana*. Other book credits include: *Montana Wild and Beautiful,* volumes one and two, *Glacier Impressions,* and *Glacier Wild and Beautiful.* John's prints appear in private collections and public venues. He also enjoys working with commercial clients.

John is affiliated with the Popular Photography / American Photo Mentor Series of workshops. He has taught photo workshops in Montana, Wyoming, Texas, Pennsylvania, Arizona, Tennessee, Fiji, and Alaska.

www.johnreddyphoto.com

*Right:* A field of irises near Haystack Butte. This conical landmark west of Great Falls was first named "Shishequaw Mountain" by members of the Lewis and Clark Expedition in July 1806.